HAL•LEONARD

JAZZ PLAY-ALONG®

k and CD for B♭, E♭, C and Bass Clef Instruments

Volume
97

BOOK

Arranged and Produced by
Howie Casey

Maybe I'm Amazed
10 Favorite Tunes

CD

ISBN 978-1-4234-6019-0

HAL•LEONARD®
CORPORATION

7777 W. BLUEMOUND RD. P.O. BOX 13819 MILWAUKEE, WI 53213

For all works contained herein:
Unauthorized copying, arranging, adapting, recording, Internet posting, public performance,
or other distribution of the printed or recorded music in this publication is an infringement of copyright.
Infringers are liable under the law.

Visit Hal Leonard Online at
www.halleonard.com

ABOUT THE SONGS

Weasel Shuffle (tracks 1/2)
This is a self-penned number based on a 24-bar blues sequence in concert G. Use the G blues and G7-C7-D7 scales in the solo section.

Maybe I'm Amazed (tracks 3/4)
A great Paul McCartney song in concert D. Use the written chart as a guide, but feel free to put your own inflections on the number. Thanks to Tim Wedlake for his excellent guitar work on this and the next track. The solo section at the end is based on Dm pentatonic and dorian scales.

Here, There and Everywhere (tracks 5/6)
A beautiful John Lennon/Paul McCartney song. Again, put your own interpretation on the melody. The fade out over a Gm to Dm should be reflective.

Comin' Home Baby (tracks 7/8)
This song by Ben Tucker is a nice little groover. It's written quite straight, so again do your own thing with the tune, as I have on most of the songs on this play-along. The solos are based around concert Dm to Gm with the descending of F/E/E♭ at the end of each chorus.

My Love (tracks 9/10)
A superb Paul McCartney song. Special thanks to my own love, Sheila, for the gorgeous back vocals. At the start of the solo section, I've given a musical nod to the great Henry McCulloch guitar solo on the original, plus a reference at the end to "Jet."

Bluebird (tracks 11/12)
I had the good fortune to play the solo on the original Paul McCartney (Wings) *Band on the Run* album, which I've re-done here. This should be played in a very laid back style. Again, thanks to my wife, Sheila, and Ray Foster for the back vocals.

Take Five (tracks 13/14)
This is a fun reggae version of the great Paul Desmond classic. Thanks to Steve Hayes for his tasty trombone. The solos are over Gm to Dm with a bridge section.

BH12 Bar Blues (tracks 15/16)
Here's another self-penned number, a basic 12-bar blues in F concert. Use of the minor pentatonic, blues, and dominant scales will do the trick. Use a tough tone with a hint of growl.

Pick Up the Pieces (tracks 17/18)
One of the all-time great instrumentals from the Average White Band. We play this as written. The solo sections are 16 bars each: 12 bars on B♭+9, 4 bars on Fm. Big thanks to both Steve on trombone and Sheila on vocals.

Yesterday (tracks 19/20)
What can you say about this song by Paul McCartney? Fabulous? Definitely! I've played this dead straight with the help of the great Steve Smith on keyboards (Room with a View studios). He played on every track.

MAYBE I'M AMAZED

Volume 97

Arranged and Produced by Howie Casey

Featured Players:

Howie Casey–Tenor Sax
Steve Hayes–Trombone
Steve Smith–Keyboards
Tim Wedlake–Guitars
Pat Davey–Bass
Paul Gill–Drums
Sheila Casey and Ray Foster–Vocals

Recorded at Room with a View studios

HOW TO USE THE CD:

Each song has <u>two</u> tracks:

1) Melody and Solo

Use this track as a learning tool for melody and solo
style and inflection.

2) Backing Tracks

Learn and perform with this accompaniment track with
the RHYTHM SECTION only.

WEASEL SHUFFLE

CD
1: WITH SAX
2: BACKING TRACKS

C VERSION

WORDS AND MUSIC BY
HOWIE CASEY

Copyright © 2008 by Howie Casey
This arrangement Copyright © 2009 by Howie Casey
All Rights Reserved   Used by Permission

HERE, THERE AND EVERYWHERE

WORDS AND MUSIC BY JOHN LENNON
AND PAUL McCARTNEY

CD
⑤: WITH SAX
⑥: BACKING TRACKS

C VERSION

Copyright © 1966 Sony/ATV Music Publishing LLC
Copyright Renewed
This arrangement Copyright © 2009 Sony/ATV Music Publishing LLC
All Rights Administered by Sony/ATV Music Publishing LLC, 8 Music Square West, Nashville, TN 37203
International Copyright Secured   All Rights Reserved

MAYBE I'M AMAZED

CD
◆ 3 : WITH SAX
◆ 4 : BACKING TRACKS

C VERSION

WORDS AND MUSIC BY
PAUL MCCARTNEY

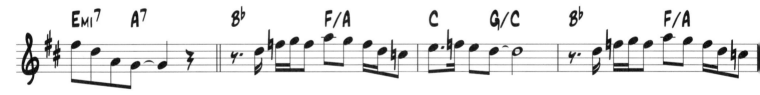

Copyright © 1970 Sony/ATV Music Publishing LLC
Copyright Renewed
This arrangement Copyright © 2009 Sony/ATV Music Publishing LLC
All Rights Administered by Sony/ATV Music Publishing LLC, 8 Music Square West, Nashville, TN 37203
International Copyright Secured   All Rights Reserved

COMIN' HOME BABY

WORDS AND MUSIC BY ROBERT DOROUGH
AND BENJAMIN TUCKER

Copyright © 1962 SINCERE MUSIC CO. and BENGLO MUSIC INC.
Copyright Renewed
This arrangement Copyright © 2009 SINCERE MUSIC CO. and BENGLO MUSIC INC.
All Rights Controlled and Administered by IRVING MUSIC, INC.
All Rights Reserved   Used by Permission

WORDS AND MUSIC BY
HOWIE CASEY

BH12 BAR BLUES

C VERSION

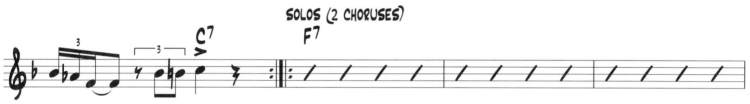

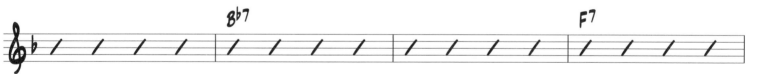

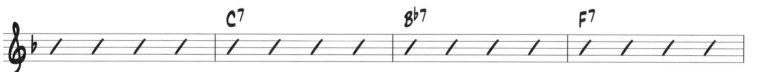

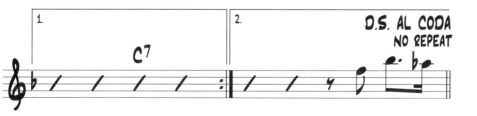

Copyright © 2008 by Howie Casey
This arrangement Copyright © 2009 by Howie Casey
All Rights Reserved   Used by Permission

MY LOVE

WORDS AND MUSIC BY
PAUL AND LINDA McCARTNEY

MEDIUM POP BALLAD

SYNTH.

© 1973 (Renewed) PAUL and LINDA McCARTNEY
This arrangement © 2009 PAUL and LINDA McCARTNEY
Administered by MPL COMMUNICATIONS, INC.
All Rights Reserved

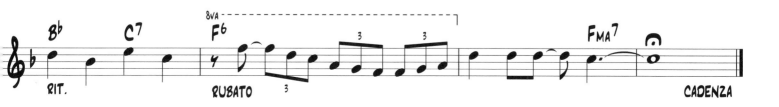

CD

11: WITH SAX
12: BACKING TRACKS

C VERSION

BLUEBIRD

WORDS AND MUSIC BY
PAUL AND LINDA MCCARTNEY

Moderato

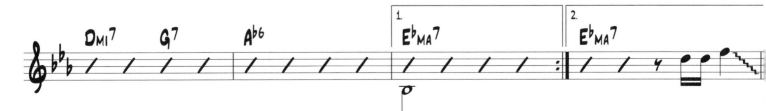

© 1974 (Renewed) PAUL and LINDA McCARTNEY
This arrangement © 2009 PAUL and LINDA McCARTNEY
Administered by MPL COMMUNICATIONS, INC.
All Rights Reserved

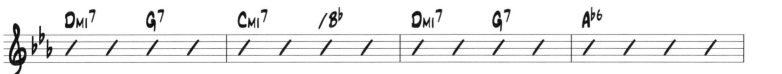

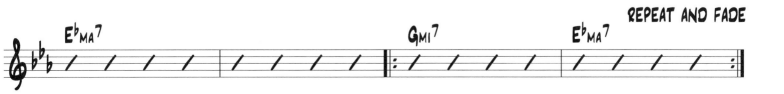

TAKE FIVE

BY PAUL DESMOND

CD

13: WITH SAX

14: BACKING TRACKS

C VERSION

© 1960 (Renewed 1988) Desmond Music Company
This arrangement © 2009 Desmond Music Company
All Rights outside the USA Controlled by Derry Music Company
International Copyright Secured   All Rights Reserved

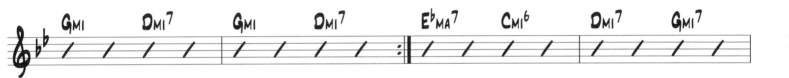

CD

C VERSION

PICK UP THE PIECES

WORDS AND MUSIC BY JAMES HAMISH STUART,
ALAN GORRIE, ROGER BALL, ROBBIE MCINTOSH,
OWEN MCINTYRE AND MALCOLM DUNCAN

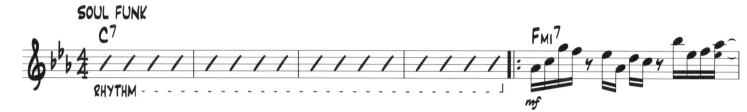

© 1974 (Renewed 2002) AVERAGE MUSIC (ASCAP)/Administered by BUG MUSIC and JOE'S SONGS, INC. (ASCAP)
This arrangement © 2009 AVERAGE MUSIC (ASCAP)/Administered by BUG MUSIC and JOE'S SONGS, INC. (ASCAP)
All Rights Reserved   Used by Permission

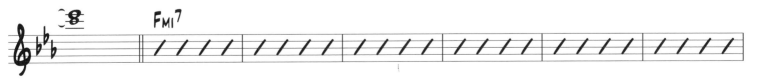

Yesterday

WORDS AND MUSIC BY JOHN LENNON
AND PAUL McCARTNEY

C VERSION

Copyright © 1965 Sony/ATV Music Publishing LLC
Copyright Renewed
This arrangement Copyright © 2009 Sony/ATV Music Publishing LLC
All Rights Administered by Sony/ATV Music Publishing LLC, 8 Music Square West, Nashville, TN 37203
International Copyright Secured   All Rights Reserved

WEASEL SHUFFLE

CD
1 : WITH SAX
2 : BACKING TRACKS

B♭ VERSION

WORDS AND MUSIC BY
HOWIE CASEY

Copyright © 2008 by Howie Casey
This arrangement Copyright © 2009 by Howie Casey
All Rights Reserved   Used by Permission

MAYBE I'M AMAZED

CD
③: WITH SAX
④: BACKING TRACKS

B♭ VERSION

WORDS AND MUSIC BY
PAUL MCCARTNEY

MEDIUM ROCK BALLAD

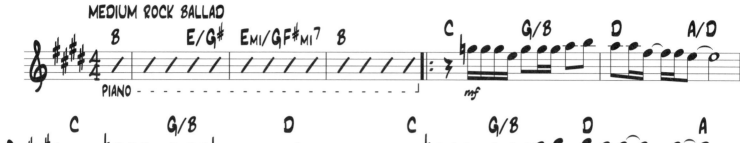

Copyright © 1970 Sony/ATV Music Publishing LLC
Copyright Renewed
This arrangement Copyright © 2009 Sony/ATV Music Publishing LLC
All Rights Administered by Sony/ATV Music Publishing LLC, 8 Music Square West, Nashville, TN 37203
International Copyright Secured All Rights Reserved

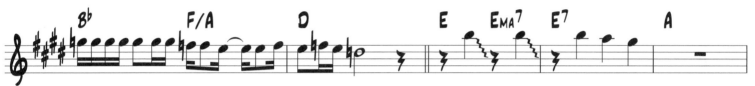

HERE, THERE AND EVERYWHERE

5: WITH SAX
6: BACKING TRACKS

WORDS AND MUSIC BY JOHN LENNON
AND PAUL MCCARTNEY

B♭ VERSION

MEDIUM ROCK BALLAD

Copyright © 1966 Sony/ATV Music Publishing LLC
Copyright Renewed
This arrangement Copyright © 2009 Sony/ATV Music Publishing LLC
All Rights Administered by Sony/ATV Music Publishing LLC, 8 Music Square West, Nashville, TN 37203
International Copyright Secured   All Rights Reserved

COMIN' HOME BABY

WORDS AND MUSIC BY ROBERT DOROUGH
AND BENJAMIN TUCKER

B♭ VERSION

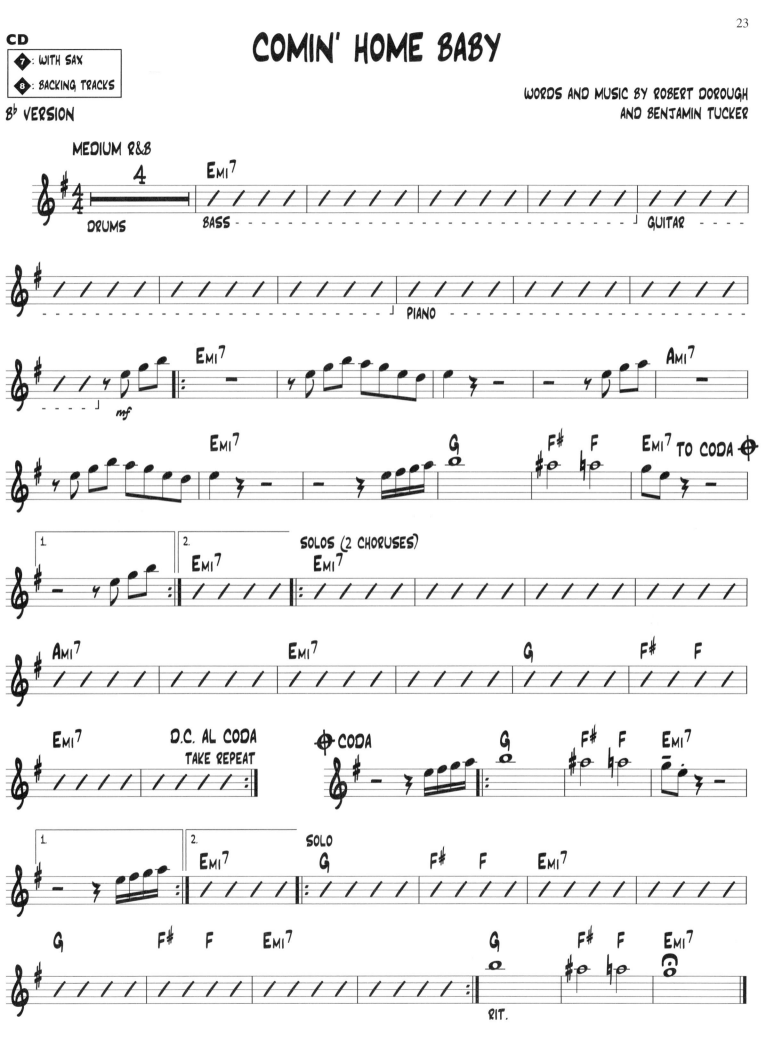

Copyright © 1962 SINCERE MUSIC CO. and BENGLO MUSIC INC.
Copyright Renewed
This arrangement Copyright © 2009 SINCERE MUSIC CO. and BENGLO MUSIC INC.
All Rights Controlled and Administered by IRVING MUSIC, INC.
All Rights Reserved   Used by Permission

MY LOVE

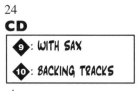

9: WITH SAX

10: BACKING TRACKS

B♭ VERSION

WORDS AND MUSIC BY
PAUL AND LINDA McCARTNEY

© 1973 (Renewed) PAUL and LINDA McCARTNEY
This arrangement © 2009 PAUL and LINDA McCARTNEY
Administered by MPL COMMUNICATIONS, INC.
All Rights Reserved

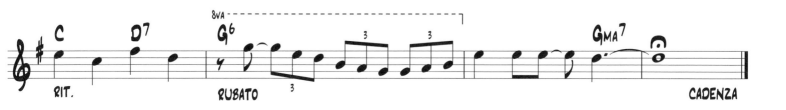

BLUEBIRD

WORDS AND MUSIC BY
PAUL AND LINDA McCARTNEY

B♭ VERSION

Moderato

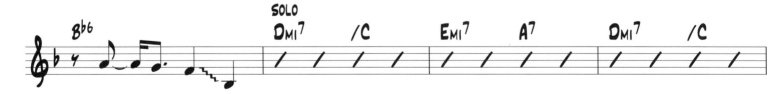

© 1974 (Renewed) PAUL and LINDA McCARTNEY
This arrangement © 2009 PAUL and LINDA McCARTNEY
Administered by MPL COMMUNICATIONS, INC.
All Rights Reserved

REPEAT AND FADE

TAKE FIVE

BY PAUL DESMOND

CD
- 13: WITH SAX
- 14: BACKING TRACKS

B♭ VERSION

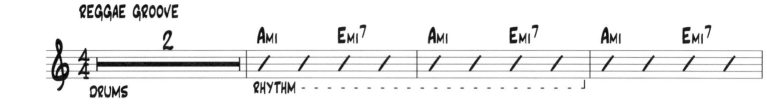

© 1960 (Renewed 1988) Desmond Music Company
This arrangement © 2009 Desmond Music Company
All Rights outside the USA Controlled by Derry Music Company
International Copyright Secured   All Rights Reserved

BH12 BAR BLUES

WORDS AND MUSIC BY
HOWIE CASEY

Copyright © 2008 by Howie Casey
This arrangement Copyright © 2009 by Howie Casey
All Rights Reserved Used by Permission

Yesterday

CD
19 : WITH SAX
20 : BACKING TRACKS

Bb VERSION

WORDS AND MUSIC BY JOHN LENNON
AND PAUL McCARTNEY

Copyright © 1965 Sony/ATV Music Publishing LLC
Copyright Renewed
This arrangement Copyright © 2009 Sony/ATV Music Publishing LLC
All Rights Administered by Sony/ATV Music Publishing LLC, 8 Music Square West, Nashville, TN 37203
International Copyright Secured   All Rights Reserved

CD

17: WITH SAX	
18: BACKING TRACKS	

B♭ VERSION

PICK UP THE PIECES

WORDS AND MUSIC BY JAMES HAMISH STUART,
ALAN GORRIE, ROGER BALL, ROBBIE McINTOSH,
OWEN McINTYRE AND MALCOLM DUNCAN

SOUL FUNK

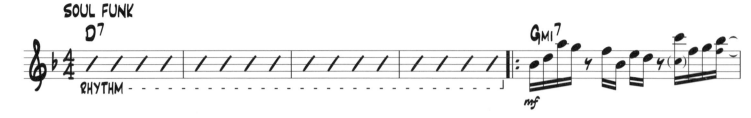

© 1974 (Renewed 2002) AVERAGE MUSIC (ASCAP)/Administered by BUG MUSIC and JOE'S SONGS, INC. (ASCAP)
This arrangement © 2009 AVERAGE MUSIC (ASCAP)/Administered by BUG MUSIC and JOE'S SONGS, INC. (ASCAP)
All Rights Reserved   Used by Permission

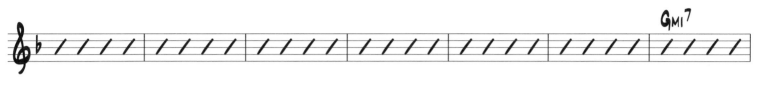

WEASEL SHUFFLE

WORDS AND MUSIC BY
HOWIE CASEY

Copyright © 2008 by Howie Casey
This arrangement Copyright © 2009 by Howie Casey
All Rights Reserved   Used by Permission

HERE, THERE AND EVERYWHERE

CD
5: WITH SAX
6: BACKING TRACKS

E♭ VERSION

WORDS AND MUSIC BY JOHN LENNON
AND PAUL McCARTNEY

Copyright © 1966 Sony/ATV Music Publishing LLC
Copyright Renewed
This arrangement Copyright © 2009 Sony/ATV Music Publishing LLC
All Rights Administered by Sony/ATV Music Publishing LLC, 8 Music Square West, Nashville, TN 37203
International Copyright Secured   All Rights Reserved

CD

MAYBE I'M AMAZED

WORDS AND MUSIC BY
PAUL McCARTNEY

E♭ VERSION

MEDIUM ROCK BALLAD

Copyright © 1970 Sony/ATV Music Publishing LLC
Copyright Renewed
This arrangement Copyright © 2009 Sony/ATV Music Publishing LLC
All Rights Administered by Sony/ATV Music Publishing LLC, 8 Music Square West, Nashville, TN 37203
International Copyright Secured All Rights Reserved

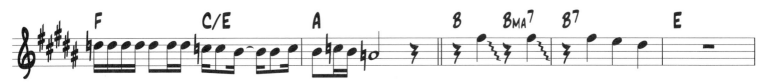

SOLO
PLAY 3X's

COMIN' HOME BABY

WORDS AND MUSIC BY ROBERT DOROUGH
AND BENJAMIN TUCKER

Copyright © 1962 SINCERE MUSIC CO. and BENGLO MUSIC INC.
Copyright Renewed
This arrangement Copyright © 2009 SINCERE MUSIC CO. and BENGLO MUSIC INC.
All Rights Controlled and Administered by IRVING MUSIC, INC.
All Rights Reserved Used by Permission

BH12 BAR BLUES

WORDS AND MUSIC BY
HOWIE CASEY

Copyright © 2008 by Howie Casey
This arrangement Copyright © 2009 by Howie Casey
All Rights Reserved   Used by Permission

CD

◆ 9 : WITH SAX

◆ 10 : BACKING TRACKS

E♭ VERSION

MY LOVE

WORDS AND MUSIC BY
PAUL AND LINDA McCARTNEY

MEDIUM POP BALLAD

SYNTH.

© 1973 (Renewed) PAUL and LINDA McCARTNEY
This arrangement © 2009 PAUL and LINDA McCARTNEY
Administered by MPL COMMUNICATIONS, INC.
All Rights Reserved

CD

11: WITH SAX
12: BACKING TRACKS

Eb VERSION

BLUEBIRD

WORDS AND MUSIC BY
PAUL AND LINDA McCARTNEY

© 1974 (Renewed) PAUL and LINDA McCARTNEY
This arrangement © 2009 PAUL and LINDA McCARTNEY
Administered by MPL COMMUNICATIONS, INC.
All Rights Reserved

TAKE FIVE

BY PAUL DESMOND

CD
13: WITH SAX
14: BACKING TRACKS

E♭ VERSION

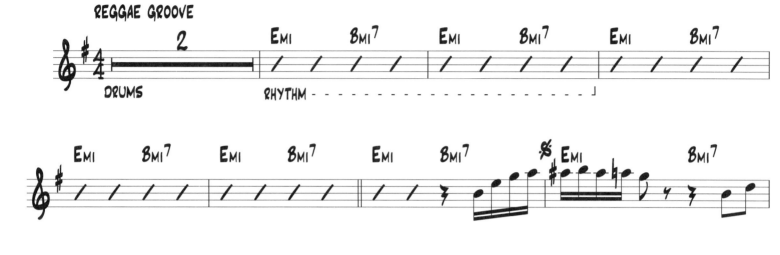

© 1960 (Renewed 1988) Desmond Music Company
This arrangement © 2009 Desmond Music Company
All Rights outside the USA Controlled by Derry Music Company
International Copyright Secured   All Rights Reserved

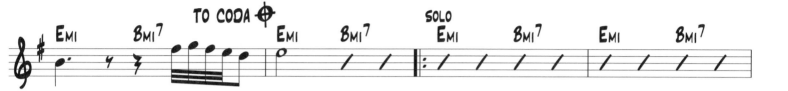

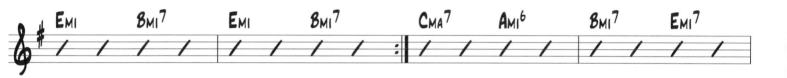

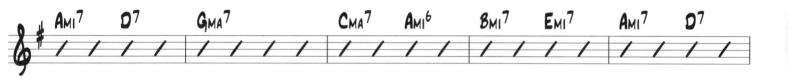

CD

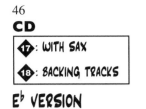

Eᵇ VERSION

PICK UP THE PIECES

WORDS AND MUSIC BY JAMES HAMISH STUART,
ALAN GORRIE, ROGER BALL, ROBBIE MCINTOSH,
OWEN MCINTYRE AND MALCOLM DUNCAN

SOUL FUNK

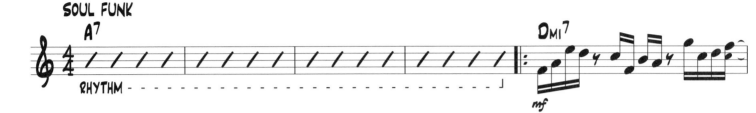

© 1974 (Renewed 2002) AVERAGE MUSIC (ASCAP)/Administered by BUG MUSIC and JOE'S SONGS, INC. (ASCAP)
This arrangement © 2009 AVERAGE MUSIC (ASCAP)/Administered by BUG MUSIC and JOE'S SONGS, INC. (ASCAP)
All Rights Reserved   Used by Permission

Yesterday

Copyright © 1965 Sony/ATV Music Publishing LLC
Copyright Renewed
This arrangement Copyright © 2009 Sony/ATV Music Publishing LLC
All Rights Administered by Sony/ATV Music Publishing LLC, 8 Music Square West, Nashville, TN 37203
International Copyright Secured   All Rights Reserved

WEASEL SHUFFLE

CD
- **1**: WITH SAX
- **2**: BACKING TRACKS

𝄢: C VERSION

WORDS AND MUSIC BY
HOWIE CASEY

MEDIUM SHUFFLE

Copyright © 2008 by Howie Casey
This arrangement Copyright © 2009 by Howie Casey
All Rights Reserved   Used by Permission

MAYBE I'M AMAZED

3 : WITH SAX
4 : BACKING TRACKS

WORDS AND MUSIC BY
PAUL McCARTNEY

C VERSION

Copyright © 1970 Sony/ATV Music Publishing LLC
Copyright Renewed
This arrangement Copyright © 2009 Sony/ATV Music Publishing LLC
All Rights Administered by Sony/ATV Music Publishing LLC, 8 Music Square West, Nashville, TN 37203
International Copyright Secured   All Rights Reserved

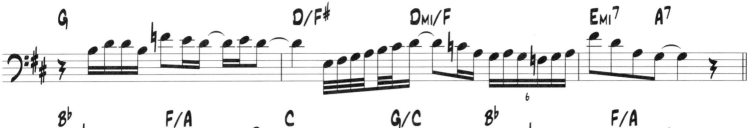

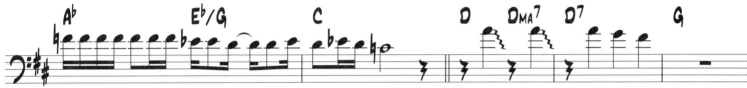

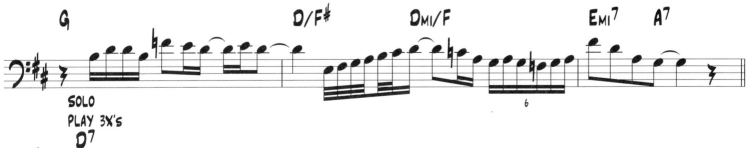

HERE, THERE AND EVERYWHERE

WORDS AND MUSIC BY JOHN LENNON
AND PAUL MCCARTNEY

Copyright © 1966 Sony/ATV Music Publishing LLC
Copyright Renewed
This arrangement Copyright © 2009 Sony/ATV Music Publishing LLC
All Rights Administered by Sony/ATV Music Publishing LLC, 8 Music Square West, Nashville, TN 37203
International Copyright Secured   All Rights Reserved

COMIN' HOME BABY

WORDS AND MUSIC BY ROBERT DOROUGH
AND BENJAMIN TUCKER

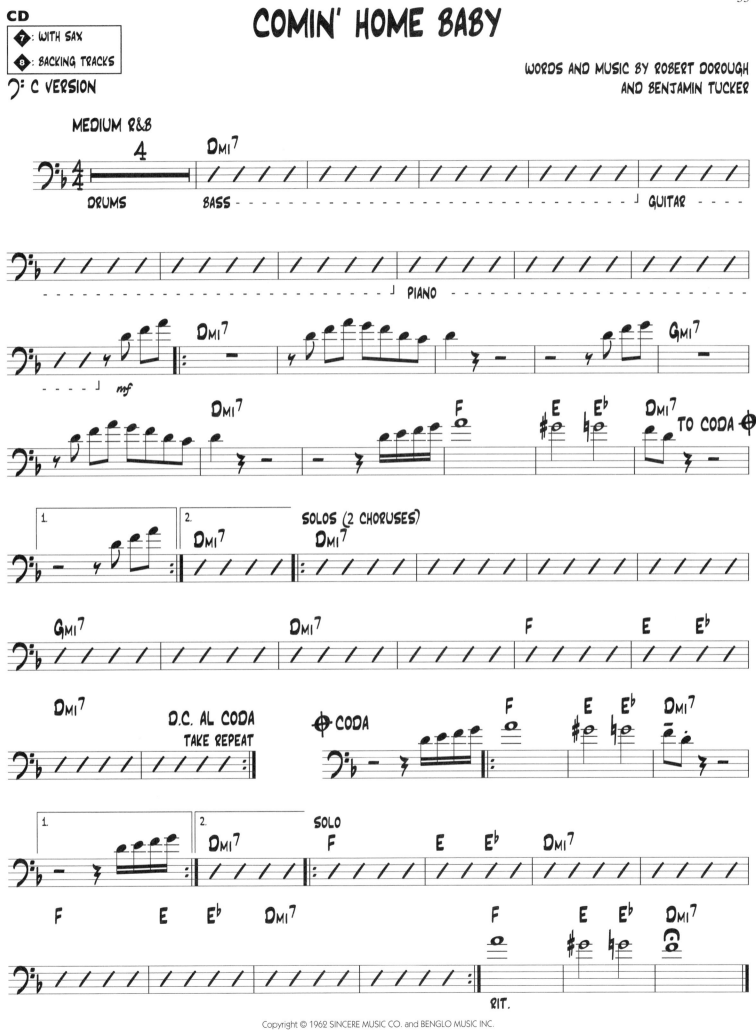

Copyright © 1962 SINCERE MUSIC CO. and BENGLO MUSIC INC.
Copyright Renewed
This arrangement Copyright © 2009 SINCERE MUSIC CO. and BENGLO MUSIC INC.
All Rights Controlled and Administered by IRVING MUSIC, INC.
All Rights Reserved   Used by Permission

MY LOVE

WORDS AND MUSIC BY
PAUL AND LINDA McCARTNEY

MEDIUM POP BALLAD

SYNTH.

© 1973 (Renewed) PAUL and LINDA McCARTNEY
This arrangement © 2009 PAUL and LINDA McCARTNEY
Administered by MPL COMMUNICATIONS, INC.
All Rights Reserved

SOLO

A TEMPO

CADENZA

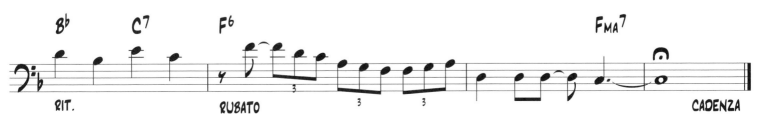

RIT.   RUBATO   CADENZA

BLUEBIRD

WORDS AND MUSIC BY
PAUL AND LINDA McCARTNEY

© 1974 (Renewed) PAUL and LINDA McCARTNEY
This arrangement © 2009 PAUL and LINDA McCARTNEY
Administered by MPL COMMUNICATIONS, INC.
All Rights Reserved

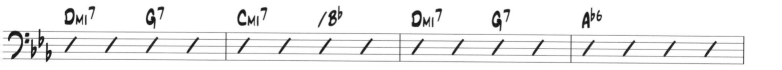

CD

13: WITH SAX

14: BACKING TRACKS

𝄢 C VERSION

TAKE FIVE

BY PAUL DESMOND

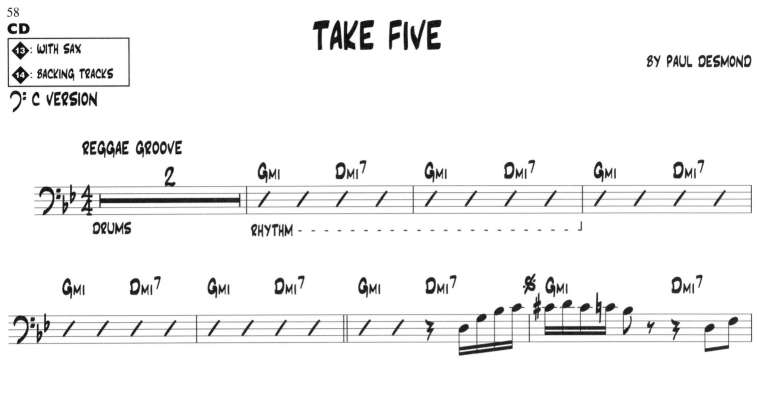

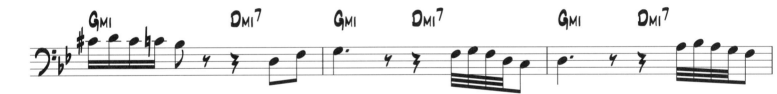

© 1960 (Renewed 1988) Desmond Music Company
This arrangement © 2009 Desmond Music Company
All Rights outside the USA Controlled by Derry Music Company
International Copyright Secured   All Rights Reserved

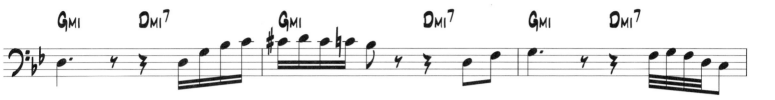

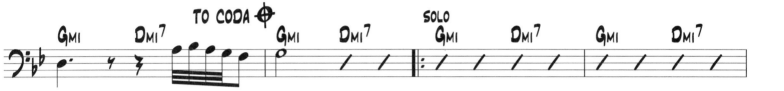

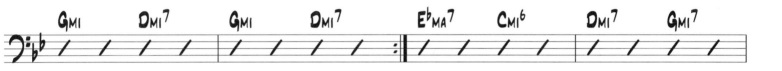

BH12 BAR BLUES

WORDS AND MUSIC BY
HOWIE CASEY

Copyright © 2008 by Howie Casey
This arrangement Copyright © 2009 by Howie Casey
All Rights Reserved   Used by Permission

Yesterday

WORDS AND MUSIC BY JOHN LENNON
AND PAUL McCARTNEY

CD
- **19** : WITH SAX
- **20** : BACKING TRACKS

C VERSION

Copyright © 1965 Sony/ATV Music Publishing LLC
Copyright Renewed
This arrangement Copyright © 2009 Sony/ATV Music Publishing LLC
All Rights Administered by Sony/ATV Music Publishing LLC, 8 Music Square West, Nashville, TN 37203
International Copyright Secured   All Rights Reserved

CD
17 : WITH SAX
18 : BACKING TRACKS

𝄢 C VERSION

PICK UP THE PIECES

WORDS AND MUSIC BY JAMES HAMISH STUART,
ALAN GORRIE, ROGER BALL, ROBBIE MCINTOSH,
OWEN MCINTYRE AND MALCOLM DUNCAN

SOUL FUNK

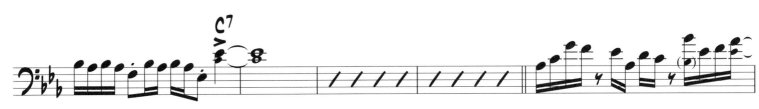

© 1974 (Renewed 2002) AVERAGE MUSIC (ASCAP)/Administered by BUG MUSIC and JOE'S SONGS, INC. (ASCAP)
This arrangement © 2009 AVERAGE MUSIC (ASCAP)/Administered by BUG MUSIC and JOE'S SONGS, INC. (ASCAP)
All Rights Reserved   Used by Permission

Presenting the Hal Leonard JAZZ PLAY-ALONG® SERIES

1. DUKE ELLINGTON
00841644 ....$16.95

2. MILES DAVIS
00841645 ....$16.95

3. THE BLUES
00841646 ....$16.99

4. JAZZ BALLADS
00841691 ....$16.99

5. BEST OF BEBOP
00841689 ....$16.99

6. JAZZ CLASSICS WITH EASY CHANGES
00841690 ....$16.99

7. ESSENTIAL JAZZ STANDARDS
00843000 ....$16.99

8. ANTONIO CARLOS JOBIM AND THE ART OF THE BOSSA NOVA
00843001 ....$16.95

9. DIZZY GILLESPIE
00843002 ....$16.99

10. DISNEY CLASSICS
00843003 ....$16.99

11. RODGERS AND HART – FAVORITES
00843004 ....$16.99

12. ESSENTIAL JAZZ CLASSICS
00843005 ....$16.99

13. JOHN COLTRANE
00843006 ....$16.95

14. IRVING BERLIN
00843007 ....$15.99

15. RODGERS & HAMMERSTEIN
00843008 ....$15.99

16. COLE PORTER
00843009 ....$15.95

17. COUNT BASIE
00843010 ....$16.95

18. HAROLD ARLEN
00843011 ....$15.95

19. COOL JAZZ
00843012 ....$15.95

20. CHRISTMAS CAROLS
00843080 ....$14.95

21. RODGERS AND HART – CLASSICS
00843014 ....$14.95

22. WAYNE SHORTER
00843015 ....$16.95

23. LATIN JAZZ
00843016 ....$16.95

24. EARLY JAZZ STANDARDS
00843017 ....$14.95

25. CHRISTMAS JAZZ
00843018 ....$16.95

26. CHARLIE PARKER
00843019 ....$16.95

27. GREAT JAZZ STANDARDS
00843020 ....$15.99

28. BIG BAND ERA
00843021 ....$15.99

29. LENNON AND McCARTNEY
00843022 ....$16.95

30. BLUES' BEST
00843023 ....$15.99

31. JAZZ IN THREE
00843024 ....$15.99

32. BEST OF SWING
00843025 ....$15.99

33. SONNY ROLLINS
00843029 ....$15.95

34. ALL TIME STANDARDS
00843030 ....$15.99

35. BLUESY JAZZ
00843031 ....$15.99

36. HORACE SILVER
00843032 ....$16.99

37. BILL EVANS
00843033 ....$16.95

38. YULETIDE JAZZ
00843034 ....$16.95

39. "ALL THE THINGS YOU ARE" & MORE JEROME KERN SONGS
00843035 ....$15.99

40. BOSSA NOVA
00843036 ....$15.99

41. CLASSIC DUKE ELLINGTON
00843037 ....$16.99

42. GERRY MULLIGAN – FAVORITES
00843038 ....$16.99

43. GERRY MULLIGAN – CLASSICS
00843039 ....$16.95

44. OLIVER NELSON
00843040 ....$16.95

45. JAZZ AT THE MOVIES
00843041 ....$15.99

46. BROADWAY JAZZ STANDARDS
00843042 ....$15.99

47. CLASSIC JAZZ BALLADS
00843043 ....$15.99

48. BEBOP CLASSICS
00843044 ....$16.99

49. MILES DAVIS – STANDARDS
00843045 ....$16.95

50. GREAT JAZZ CLASSICS
00843046 ....$15.99

51. UP-TEMPO JAZZ
00843047 ....$15.99

52. STEVIE WONDER
00843048 ....$15.95

53. RHYTHM CHANGES
00843049 ....$15.99

54. "MOONLIGHT IN VERMONT" & OTHER GREAT STANDARDS
00843050 ....$15.99

55. BENNY GOLSON
00843052 ....$15.95

56. "GEORGIA ON MY MIND" & OTHER SONGS BY HOAGY CARMICHAEL
00843056 ....$15.99

57. VINCE GUARALDI
00843057 ....$16.99

58. MORE LENNON AND McCARTNEY
00843059 ....$15.99

59. SOUL JAZZ
00843060 ....$15.99

60. DEXTER GORDON
00843061 ....$15.95

61. MONGO SANTAMARIA
00843062 ....$15.95

62. JAZZ-ROCK FUSION
00843063 ....$14.95

63. CLASSICAL JAZZ
00843064 ....$14.95

64. TV TUNES
00843065 ....$14.95

65. SMOOTH JAZZ
00843066 ....$16.99

66. A CHARLIE BROWN CHRISTMAS
00843067 ....$16.99

67. CHICK COREA
00843068 ....$15.95

68. CHARLES MINGUS
00843069 ....$16.95

69. CLASSIC JAZZ
00843071 ....$15.99

70. THE DOORS
00843072 ....$14.95

71. COLE PORTER CLASSICS
00843073 ....$14.95

72. CLASSIC JAZZ BALLADS
00843074 ....$15.99

73. JAZZ/BLUES
00843075 ....$14.95

74. BEST JAZZ CLASSICS
00843076 ....$15.99

75. PAUL DESMOND
00843077 ....$14.95

76. BROADWAY JAZZ BALLADS
00843078 ....$15.99

77. JAZZ ON BROADWAY
00843079 ....$15.99

78. STEELY DAN
00843070 ....$14.99

79. MILES DAVIS – CLASSICS
00843081 ....$15.99

80. JIMI HENDRIX
00843083 ....$15.99

81. FRANK SINATRA – CLASSICS
00843084 ....$15.99

82. FRANK SINATRA – STANDARDS
00843085 ....$15.99

83. ANDREW LLOYD WEBBER
00843104 ....$14.95

84. BOSSA NOVA CLASSICS
00843105 ....$14.95

85. MOTOWN HITS
00843109 ....$14.95

86. BENNY GOODMAN
00843110 ....$14.95

87. DIXIELAND
00843111 ....$14.95

88. DUKE ELLINGTON FAVORITES
00843112 ....$14.95

89. IRVING BERLIN FAVORITES
00843113 ....$14.95

90. THELONIOUS MONK CLASSICS
00841262 ....$16.99

91. THELONIOUS MONK FAVORITES
00841263 ....$16.99

92. LEONARD BERNSTEIN
00450134 ....$14.99

93. DISNEY FAVORITES
00843142 ....$14.99

94. RAY
00843143 ....$14.95

95. JAZZ AT THE LOUNGE
00843144 ....$14.99

96. LATIN JAZZ STANDARDS
00843145 ....$14.99

97. MAYBE I'M AMAZED
00843148 ....$14.99

98. DAVE FRISHBERG
00843149 ....$15.99

99. SWINGING STANDARDS
00843150 ....$14.99

100. LOUIS ARMSTRONG
00740423 ....$15.99

101. BUD POWELL
00843152 ....$14.99

102. JAZZ POP
00843153 ....$14.99

103. ON GREEN DOLPHIN STREET & OTHER JAZZ CLASSICS
00843154 ....$14.99

104. ELTON JOHN
00843155 ....$14.99

105. SOULFUL JAZZ
00843151 ....$14.99

106. SLO' JAZZ
00843117 ....$14.99

107. MOTOWN CLASSICS
00843116 ....$14.99

111. COOL CHRISTMAS
00843162 ....$15.99

For use with all B-flat, E-flat, Bass Clef and C instruments, the Jazz Play-Along® Series is the ultimate learning tool for all jazz musicians. With musician-friendly lead sheets, melody cues, and other split-track choices on the included CD, these first-of-a-kind packages help you master improvisation while playing some of the greatest tunes of all time. FOR STUDY, each tune includes a split track with: melody cue with proper style and inflection • professional rhythm tracks • choruses for soloing • removable bass part • removable piano part. FOR PERFORMANCE, each tune also has: an additional full stereo accompaniment track (no melody) • additional choruses for soloing.

Prices, contents, and availability subject to change without notice.

FOR MORE INFORMATION, SEE YOUR LOCAL MUSIC DEALER, OR WRITE TO:

HAL•LEONARD®
CORPORATION
7777 W. BLUEMOUND RD. P.O. BOX 13819
MILWAUKEE, WISCONSIN 53213

Visit Hal Leonard online at
www.halleonard.com
for complete songlists.

0809